RACE TO THE POLE

MIKE GOULD

Contents

D0258534

A deadly race

Just over one hundred years ago, two men took part in a deadly race. One man and his team would not survive.

Where did the race take place? And what was the goal?

Look at this map. It shows a land that hardly anyone knew at that time: Antarctica.

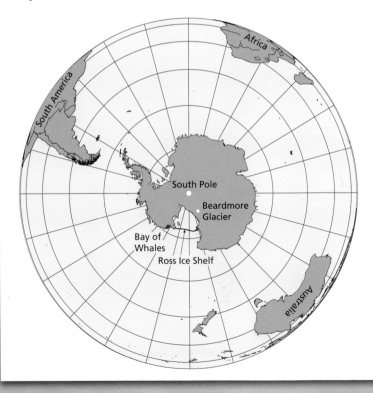

The South Pole

Within Antarctica is the South Pole. It is the southern-most point on the earth, opposite the North Pole.

The average temperature is about minus fifty degrees. That is COLD.

Antarctica has six months of daylight and six months of darkness. At the South Pole in December, there is no night – just daylight all the time.

The South Pole was the place our two men wanted to reach.

Their names?

Robert Falcon Scott, from England, and Roald Amundsen, from Norway.

Antarctica is 99% covered by ice and snow.
We call Antarctica and the area around it, "the Antarctic".

Explorers

Other explorers had wanted to find out more about this remote land, its geography and its wildlife.

James Clarke Ross (1800–1862)

Who was he? An officer in the British Navy.

What did he do? He explored volcanoes, seas and coastlines, putting them on a map of Antarctica for the first time.

How close did he get to the South Pole? About five hundred miles away.

What stopped him? His ships were faced with a huge wall of ice seventy metres high. This was later named "The Ross Ice Shelf".

Ernest Shackleton (1874–1922)

Who was he? A British explorer who first visited the Antarctic in 1901. He fell ill and had to return home, but he wanted to go back.

What did he do? In 1909, he and three others got within nearly one hundred miles of the South Pole.

Why didn't they reach it? They ran out of food and only just made it back.

 Did you know? Years later, Shackleton's ship sank in the Antarctic. The crew had to row eight hundred miles through stormy seas to safety.

Captain Scott

Scott was a Navy captain.

He had already led one **expedition** to try and reach the South Pole. He wanted to try again.

He needed:

- a team of men (more than sixty altogether)
- food and supplies for at least two years
- equipment, such as cameras
- transport (sledges, with dogs and ponies to pull them)
- … and a ship!

> **expedition**
> an organised voyage

Scott's ship, the Terra Nova

> **Did you know?** Terra Nova is Latin for "new land".

More than one hundred companies gave equipment and supplies to help the expedition.

The British government gave Scott £20 000 (about one and a half million pounds in today's money). They hoped he would make important scientific discoveries.

Supplies of Fry's Cocoa & Chocolate were given to Scott's team.

Equipment and supplies for the journey were carefully written down.

Who was Amundsen?

Roald Amundsen
was born in 1872.

Unlike Scott, he had always wanted to be an
explorer.

His mother had wanted him to be a doctor,
but when she died he gave up his studies.

By 1910, he was an experienced explorer.

At first, he wasn't really bothered about the South
Pole. He wanted to be the first to the *North* Pole.

Then he heard that someone else, the American Robert Peary, had got to the North Pole first. So he decided to head south instead – for Antarctica.

His decision would change history.

Amundsen and his team left Norway in August 1910 aboard his ship, *Fram*.

Fram means "forward".

It was only then that he told his crew they were going to the South Pole.

Why do you think he hadn't told them earlier?

Did you know?

Many people now wonder if Peary really did reach the North Pole. He had no proof and they think his calculations may have been wrong.

The race is on

Australia was the stopping point on the way to Antarctica.

While Scott was there with his team in October 1910, he received a telegram.

It was from Amundsen.

> Beg to inform you Fram proceeding
> Antarctic – Amundsen

This was a big surprise to Scott.

But he knew Amundsen was a great explorer and that, like Scott, he wanted to be the first to reach a place no one else had ever been.

Scott finally arrived in the Antarctic after an awful journey. Terrible storms had killed some of the dogs and ponies, and had almost sunk the ship.

It was now December 1910. Scott and his team needed a year to get ready for the expedition to the South Pole, but they had arrived much later than planned.

This meant less time to prepare while the weather was good.

Two weeks later, Amundsen's ship landed at the Bay of Whales.

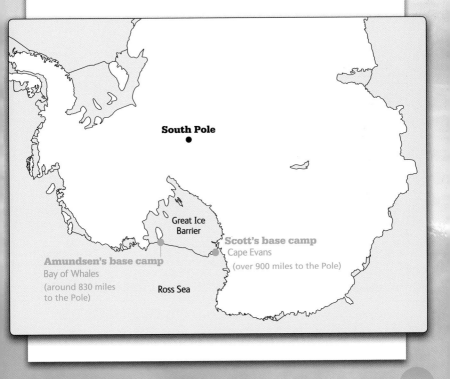

South Pole

Great Ice Barrier

Scott's base camp
Cape Evans
(over 900 miles to the Pole)

Amundsen's base camp
Bay of Whales
(around 830 miles to the Pole)

Ross Sea

Scientific work

Some of Scott's team were scientists. Their job was to collect examples of different forms of wildlife. They found things that had never been seen before.

Here is a creature like a large crab or woodlouse, discovered during the expedition.

Three members of the team went to collect emperor penguin eggs so they could study their development.

But it was the middle of the winter, and a storm blew away their tent. After five terrible weeks, they just managed to get back to base – with only three eggs.

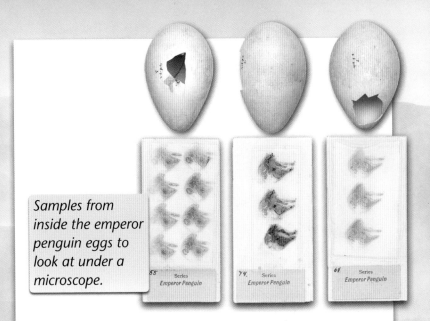

Samples from inside the emperor penguin eggs to look at under a microscope.

Setting up depots

Depots were camps where food and equipment would be left so that when Scott and his men finally set out for the Pole, there would be supplies for them on the way there and back.

One Ton Depot was the last camp they would arrive at on the way back from the Pole.

Bad weather meant that Scott had to set up One Ton Depot further from the Pole than he had planned. This would prove fatal for his final journey.

Food and clothing

Diet was very important. The men needed to take food that would give them lots of energy for the journey. But the food also had to be light and easy to carry.

Pemmican was a mixture of dried beef and beef fat. It didn't taste very nice!

BOVRIL PEMMICAN

A HIGHLY SUSTAINING FOOD CONSISTING OF BEEF
PROTEIN AND BEEF FAT WITH ADDED YEAST EXTRACT
A CONCENTRATE FOR USE IN COLD REGIONS

NET WEIGHT 1 lb.

BOVRIL LIMITED · LONDON · E.C.1 · ENGLAND

Clothing was vital, too. Scott's men had clothes made of fur and animal skin. They wore lots of woollen layers underneath. This made them sweat.

If you sweat, it lets cold and damp into the layers of your clothing.

Here is Scott at base camp, surrounded by all sorts of clothing and supplies.

Today, we have fabrics which keep out the cold, but also let your sweat escape.

Amundsen's choices

Unlike Scott, Amundsen did not bother with the scientific work. Instead, he and his team would focus on getting to the South Pole first.

He made sure his depots were well stocked. He and his team would have less to carry, but plenty of supplies when they needed them.

He had another advantage: his base camp was about seventy miles nearer the South Pole than Scott's, so he wouldn't have as far to travel.

What other differences were there?

Amundsen's men wore loose-fitting animal furs and skins, without the heavy woollens that Scott preferred.

He also used only dogs and skis for travelling.

They would kill some of their dogs on the journey and use them as food. Amundsen and his men didn't want to do this, but they knew it would mean less to carry and fewer dogs to feed later.

Scott had brought ponies and motor sledges, as well as dogs. But the sledges kept breaking down.

And the decision to use ponies turned out to be a mistake.

To the Pole!

Scott sets off

On 1 November 1911, sixteen men left the base camp at Cape Evans.

The group included the men who would go on with Scott towards the South Pole. But Scott hadn't yet told them who that would be.

The other men's job was to help carry supplies for the final team. They also had to set up more depots for use on the way back.

It was like a nightmare from the start.

First, they had to wait for warmer weather for the ponies. This meant that they started almost two weeks later than Amundsen.

Scott's team, with sledges, dogs and ponies, all moved at different speeds. This slowed them down, as the fastest had to wait for the slowest.

Yet they all had to face the same ice-blocks, hidden **crevasses** and very strong winds.

crevasses
deep cracks in the ice

Amundsen on the way

Amundsen had left for the South Pole with his men, and fifty dogs, on 20 October 1911.

He had picked his men himself.

His men knew from the start who would be in the final group to head for the Pole. They included a skiing champion and two expert dog-drivers.

The dogs were ideal for Antarctic travel.

Capt. R. Amundsen
Arctic Explorer

Copyright 1906
By C. L. Andrews

Amundsen had taken dogs with him before, on a trip in 1906. He knew they could cope well.

Bad news for the ponies

For Scott's team, it was soon clear that the ponies were not suitable because they slipped on the ice and sank in the snow.

The man in charge of them, Captain Oates, was unhappy about the ponies' treatment and argued with Scott.

Sadly, the ponies had to be shot. Some of them were left at a depot as meat for the return journey.

Scott's team goes ahead

After crossing the Beardmore Glacier, Scott divided his team.

He chose these men to go with him to the Pole:

Captain Oates

Petty Officer Edgar Evans

Edward Wilson

Henry "Birdie" Bowers.

From then on, they pulled the sledges themselves. They often sank up to their waists in the soft snow.

Scott and his men were now about one hundred and fifty miles from the South Pole.

The end was in sight.

Then, on 6 January, they passed the point that Ernest Shackleton had reached in 1909 before he was forced to turn back.

It was a great moment. They believed that no man or woman on earth had ever been as far south before.

They were wrong.

Did you know? Scott had planned to take only three men with him to the Pole, but at the last moment added Bowers. This meant there was less food to go round.

It took Scott and his team another ten days of hard work to cover the remaining one hundred miles to the Pole.

On 16 January, they were just one day away from reaching the Pole.

Then Bowers spotted something. It was a flag left by other explorers.

That could only mean one thing. Amundsen and his men were ahead of them.

By now, Scott and his men had **frostbite**. On 17 January, in temperatures of minus thirty degrees, they arrived at the Pole.

There, they found a tent.

It was Amundsen's.

Inside was a letter from Amundsen, addressed to Scott. He and his men had arrived on 14 December 1911. That was thirty-four days earlier!

Scott was very disappointed. He wrote:

> The Pole. Yes. But under very different circumstances from those expected ...

frostbite
extreme cold can cause fingers, ears, toes and noses to rot or even fall off

These two photos sum up what had happened.

The one on this page shows Amundsen and his men, proudly standing beside their Pole tent, with the Norwegian flag flying above it.

This one tells a very different story.

It shows Scott and his men, standing beside the Union Jack.

Their faces show how disappointed they were.

And they still had to face the journey back.

It was time to leave.

Scott and his men were already weak, as they had used up so much energy pulling the sledges.

The team was also low on food, as they had only planned for four men.

They probably had **hypothermia**, too, which would have made them light-headed and perhaps unable to think properly.

It was a very dangerous mix.

hypothermia
when the body's temperature drops so low that it can no longer work properly

Ahead of them was an ordeal far worse than the journey on the way out.

The weather was even more terrible. The Antarctic winter seemed to have arrived early.

And some of the men were sick, especially Evans.

The death of Evans

Edgar Evans had been the strongest of the five men in the final group. But he was also the biggest.

This meant he needed more food and was the first to starve. He also had a cut on his hand that would not heal due to the extreme cold.

He was soon unable to pull a sledge and had frostbite on his nose.

After a bad fall, his condition got worse and worse.

On 17 February, he collapsed as the team crossed the Beardmore Glacier.

He had fallen behind the others and when they found him, Scott said he had a "wild look in his eyes".

They loaded him onto a sledge and pulled him to the nearest tent, but he died that night.

The next morning, the remaining four left the glacier. They were forced to leave Evans's body behind.

It has never been found.

"I am just going outside ..."

Scott, Oates, Bowers and Wilson went on.

They were now on the Ross Ice Shelf, but conditions were no better.

They couldn't believe how unlucky they were.

The weather was very bad indeed, even worse than normal.

It was the middle of March. The men were trapped inside their tent, unable to leave.

Outside, there was a blizzard.

Oates was very sick. He had frostbite so badly that he could hardly walk.

He knew he was holding the others back and there was no way they could look after him.
So, either on his 32nd birthday or the day before it, he walked out of the tent into the storm.

Scott wrote Oates's final words in his diary.
Oates told the others:

"I am just going outside and may be some time."

He never came back.

The end

The remaining three carried on for a few more days. They made their last camp on 19 March 1912.

After 21 March, we know from Scott's diaries that the men were unable even to leave their tent.

The blizzard still raged.

They were just eleven miles from the One Ton Depot and safety. If the depot had been where Scott had planned, they would have reached it.

They were ill, suffering from severe frostbite and hardly able to move.

They began to write letters to their friends and families.

Scott's last diary entry, on 29 March 1912, is now famous:

> We shall stick it out to the end, but we are getting weaker of course and the end cannot be far. It seems a pity, but I do not think I can write more –
>
> R. Scott

For God's sake, look after our people.

The three men died around this time.

Did you know? You can see Scott's diary in the British Library in London.

It would be over seven months before the tent and the bodies were discovered.

Several expeditions led by members of the team back at Scott's base set out to try and find them, but each time they were driven back by the weather.

By October 1912, winter was fading and finally a search party found Scott's tent and the three bodies.

The search party collected their letters and belongings, and returned to base camp.

The bodies were left at the spot.

THE INNER TENT IN WHICH CAPTAIN SCOTT AND HIS TWO COMPANIONS WERE DISCOVERED

This illustration is from a direct photograph taken by a member of the relief party which found Captain Scott's tent on November 12, 1912. The view shows the inner lining of the tent supported on its poles. Commander Evans in his despatch from Christchurch, New Zealand, on February 13 last, said that "the search party found the tent half covered with snow. The sledge with the gear was completely covered, the tent was well spread, and the inner tent was in place on the poles. The bodies were identified, the inner tent was placed over them, and a large cairn of snow was erected"

A huge **cairn** of ice was built and placed over their bodies, with a cross on top.

cairn

a mound of stones or ice blocks,
often made as a memorial

The news reaches England

By March 1912, the world knew that Amundsen had won the race.

Then, almost a whole year later, news of Scott's death was revealed.

The British newspapers were full of the story, painting Scott as a noble hero.

There was a huge memorial service at St Paul's Cathedral, attended by King George the Fifth.

People were very proud of what Scott had done and of how brave he had been.

IN MEMORY OF THE ANTARCTIC HEROES, THE LATE CAPTAIN SCOTT AND HIS GALLANT COMRADES, WHO PERISHED MARCH, 1912, AT THE SOUTH POLE.

Beyond the track of human life,
Away through an endless waste,
The end achieved, but lo! sad news
Of death most bravely faced.

Beyond the woes of earthly strife,
Away to an endless rest—
A destiny we may not choose
Has done its worst, and best.

Some said that Amundsen had not acted fairly by misleading Scott about his plans, and that he had had better luck.

What was the truth?

Yes, Scott did have some bad luck in terms of weather, but he also made big mistakes – taking ponies, for example, and adding an extra man for the final journey to the Pole.

Amundsen's planning and preparation were probably better.

Life after the South Pole

Amundsen carried on exploring.

He led an expedition to the North Pole in 1926 and it is believed that he may have been the first to reach there, too.

Then, in 1928, while he was in an aircraft searching for some lost explorers in the Arctic, he crashed into the sea.

His body has never been found, but his achievements will never be forgotten.

A memorial to Amundsen in Norway.

Memories

Today, a memorial to Scott can still be seen in Antarctica.

It contains these words by the poet Tennyson:

"To **strive**, to seek, to find, and not to **yield**."

There is also a statue of Scott in New Zealand, close to Antarctica.

strive
try very hard

yield
give up

Antarctica today

The strongest winds and the lowest temperatures in the world are found in Antarctica.

It is, in fact, the driest continent on Earth and is called a "polar desert".

In 1956, a centre for study and exploration was opened. It was called "The Amundsen-Scott South Pole station".

Over two hundred people visit the centre and stay there each summer.

But how many realise the importance of Scott's work?

Four hundred of the animal specimens discovered by Scott's team had never been seen before. When the men's bodies were found, there were also several fossils in their tent. One dated back 250 million years!

His men were also the first to gather detailed information about weather patterns in Antarctica.

Did you know?

Now you can fly into Antarctica for organised holidays and tours!

Cape Evans Hut, where Scott began his journey, is still there, over one hundred years later.

Is there anywhere left to explore?

Today, we have explored most of the earth. But there are still some places we know little about.

The Mariana Trench

This is the deepest place in the oceans – nearly seven miles deep.

The water pressure is so strong that it is almost impossible for humans to explore.

Even with **ROVs**, finding information has proved very, very difficult.

Until recently people believed nothing could live there. It was said that more was known about life on the moon! Now we do know there is life in the trench: tiny creatures or plants that can survive without light.

ROVs

Remote Observation Vehicles, used to film in places where it is too dangerous – or impossible – for humans to go

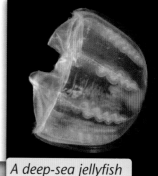

A deep-sea jellyfish

The earth's core

Another place we can't get near is the earth's core. The pressure and temperature are just too high.

The deepest we have gone – and that's just with a drill – is less than eight miles down into the earth's crust. That is less than 0.4% of the way to the core!

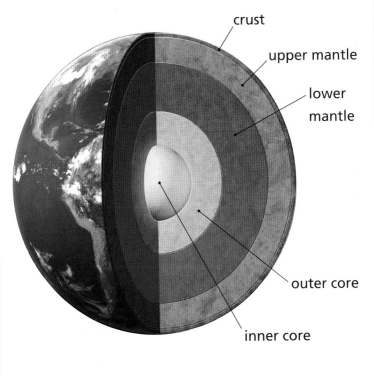

crust

upper mantle

lower mantle

outer core

inner core

Where else do you think people might explore in your lifetime?

Reader challenge

Word hunt

1. On page 4, find an adjective that means "far away".

2. On page 6, find a noun that means "journey".

3. On page 39, find an adjective that means "full of courage".

Text sense

4. Why were Scott's men unable to leave their tent? (page 34)

5. Why do you think the search party left the bodies where they found them? (page 36)

6. What mistakes did Scott make in his planning? (page 39)

7. Why is Antarctica called a "polar desert"? (page 42)

8. Why was Scott's journey so important, even though he didn't win the race to the Pole? (page 43)

Your views

9 Do you think it might be true that Amundsen had been unfair and misled Scott about his plans? Give reasons.

10 Would you like to visit Antarctica? Give reasons.

Spell it

With a partner, look at these words and then cover them up.

- explore
- expedition
- extreme

Take it in turns for one of you to read the words aloud. The other person has to try and spell each word. Check your answers, then swap over.

Try it

Read pages 28 and 29 again. With a partner, imagine you are Scott and Evans on their way home. Make a freeze-frame showing a scene from your journey.

William Collins's dream of knowledge for all began with the publication of his first book in 1819. A self-educated mill worker, he not only enriched millions of lives, but also founded a flourishing publishing house. Today, staying true to this spirit, Collins books are packed with inspiration, innovation and practical expertise. They place you at the centre of a world of possibility and give you exactly what you need to explore it.

Collins. Freedom to teach.

Published by Collins Education
An imprint of HarperCollins*Publishers*
77–85 Fulham Palace Road, Hammersmith, London W6 8JB
In association with the Natural History Museum.

Browse the complete Collins Education catalogue at **www.collinseducation.com**

Text by Mike Gould
© HarperCollins*Publishers* Limited 2012
Based on the book *Scott's Last Expedition* by Steven Parker, © Natural History Museum, London, 2011

Series consultants: Alan Gibbons and Natalie Packer

10 9 8 7 6 5 4 3 2 1
ISBN 978-0-00-750293-6

All rights reserved. No part of this publication may be reproduced, stored in a retrieval system, or transmitted in any form or by any means, electronic, mechanical, photocopying, recording or otherwise, without the prior written permission of the Publisher or a licence permitting restricted copying in the United Kingdom issued by the Copyright Licensing Agency Ltd, 90 Tottenham Court Road, London W1T 4LP.

British Library Cataloguing in Publication Data.
A catalogue record for this publication is available from the British Library.

Commissioned by Catherine Martin

Edited and project-managed by Sue Chapple

Picture research and proofreading by Grace Glendinning

Design and typesetting by Jordan Publishing Design Limited

Cover design by Paul Manning

Acknowledgements

The publishers would like to thank the students and teachers of the following schools for their help in trialling the Read On series:

Southfields Academy, London
Queensbury School, Queensbury, Bradford
Langham C of E Primary School, Langham, Rutland
Ratton School, Eastbourne, East Sussex
Northfleet School for Girls, North Fleet, Kent
Westergate Community School, Chichester, West Sussex
Bottesford C of E Primary School, Bottesford, Nottinghamshire
Woodfield Academy, Redditch, Worcestershire
St Richard's Catholic College, Bexhill, East Sussex

The publishers gratefully acknowledge the permission granted to reproduce pictures in this book. While every effort has been made to trace and contact copyright holders, where this has not been possible the publishers will be pleased to make the necessary arrangements at the first opportunity.

The publisher would like to thank the following for permission to reproduce pictures in these pages (t = top, b = bottom, c = centre, l = left, r = right):

p 2 Alfonso de Tomas/Shutterstock, p 4 Look and Learn/ The Bridgeman Art Library, p 5 Hulton Archive/Getty Image, p 6bm 21, 22–23 Popperfoto/Getty Images, p 7r Mary Evans/Grenville Collins Postcard Collection, p 8, 36 & 38 Illustrated London News/Mary Evans, p 9 Oesterreichsches Volkshochschularchiv/Imagno/ Getty Images, pp 16–17 General Photographic Agency/ Getty Images, pp 18–29 Dimos/Shutterstock, p 20 C.L. Andrews/CORBIS, p 24 North Wind Picture Archives/ Alamy, p 26 Mary Evans Picture Library, p 27 & 33 Archive Pics/Alamy, pp 28–29 Ethan Welty/Getty Images, p 39 The Print Collector/Alamy, p 40 blickwinkel/Alamy, p 41t David Ball/Alamy, p 41b Claver Carroll/Getty Images, p 42 AFP/ Getty Images, p 43 Chris Walker/Chicago Tribune/MCT via Getty Images, p 44 Sonke Johnsen/Visuals Unlimited, Inc./ Science Photo Library, p 45 Andrea Danti/Shutterstock

With particular thanks to the Natural History Museum for help with the following images:

p 6t 19XX.2.5103, p 7l MS127, p 14t 19XX.4.3470, p 15 H Pointing photograph, Pennell collection 1975.289.35, p 30 H Ponting photograph, Pennell collection, 1975.289.114, p 37 19XX.2.5093 © Canterbury Museum, New Zealand.

pp 11–13 © Natural History Museum, London

p 14b © New Zealand Antarctic Heritage Trust

p 35 © The British Library Board. By permission of the estate of R F Scott and the British Library.